GET PAID USING YOUR VOICE

Get Found, Get Heard, and Get Hired!

Bill DeWees

Hi there.

You're reading this book because you want to learn how to become a voice-over, or VO, artist and make a great living from the comfort of your own home. That's great. Thanks for joining me. Before we begin, I want to be upfront and honest with you. I have an ulterior motive.

I created this book so that you would read it, decide I know what I'm talking about, and hire me to give you extra help to become a VO artist. Don't worry. Everything you need to become a successful VO artist is included in this book. I hate bait-and-switch schemes, and haven't left anything out. It is simply my hope that you will turn to me for even greater success once you get going. And to show you I know what I'm talking about, I'm putting all of my knowledge into this book. As one wise person once said, if you want people to believe you can help them, help them.

Sound good? Keep reading.

CONTENTS

WHO AM I AND WHY SHOULD YOU LISTEN TO ME?

My name is Bill DeWees, and I have been a professional, and highly-paid, VO artist for the past 17 years. I have recorded thousands of projects for many of the world's leading brands, including Walmart, Coca-Cola, Disney, Chevrolet, Apple, American Express, United Airlines, Kellogg, and much more.

From my cozy home studio in America's Midwest, I work with businesses all over the world recording radio and TV commercials, brand anthems, explainer videos, training and instruction projects, video game characters, trailers, promos and more. The work is always interesting, and I never get bored. For some examples of my voice-over work visit my website at BillDeWees.com.

HOW DID I GET STARTED?

From the time I was twelve I wanted to be a radio DJ. I would borrow my sister's cassette recorder and lock myself in my bedroom with my records and read from the newspaper. I studied Communications in college and got a job in radio. I was a morning personality, a program director, and eventually a station manager for a university owned non-profit, where I also taught communications and business courses. With my MBA in hand, I left radio and academia in 2005 and went to work for a business consulting firm, where I was later recruited to an instructional design firm. I was downsized from that job in 2006. Faced with the fear and uncertainty of not knowing how I was going to take care of my family, I made the switch to recording freelance voice-over work, and haven't looked back.

The leap to VO artist was my hail Mary pass, and it paid off.

I tell you all of this not to brag, but to show you that I know what I'm doing. The things I'm about to teach you aren't theory or something I pulled from a book. These are the actual tested techniques I used to go from voice-over zero to voice-over hero and build a successful and sustainable six-figure business.

I also made a lot of mistakes along the way, and I don't want you to make those same mistakes.

WHY NOW IS THE BEST TIME TO BE A FREELANCE VO ARTIST

Back in the 90s I toyed with the idea of becoming a freelance voice-over artist. But times were different back then. Here's how you became a professional VO artist back then: You produced a professional demo. Then you got an agent. Your agent was the gatekeeper to the work, and the vast majority of good-paying work came from agents.

Once you had an agent, you then had to audition over and over and over again. In person. For me, this meant driving two hours round trip into the city to audition. If you were lucky enough to get the job, that meant another half day into the city to do the project. Because I already had a successful career, not to mention a wife and three kids, it just wasn't feasible for me. So I put that dream aside.

Fast forward to 2006 and it was the beginning of VO becoming democratized by the Internet. You could pay an annual fee and get access to auditions, bypassing the traditional agent route. I went at it full throttle, marketing myself all hours of the day and night. Once I got traction, I got jobs immediately, and once it started growing it didn't stop. You might recall that 2006 was right at the beginning of a recession. I didn't even think about the recession. I was too busy!

These days you don't need an agent. Thanks to advanced and affordable hardware and software, you don't need to audition in person. You don't even need a professional demo, at least in the beginning. This is absolutely the best time on the planet to get started in freelance voice-over.

Maybe you were downsized like me. Maybe you're stressed out and looking for a career change. Maybe you are looking for something to do in your retirement, or maybe you just want to work from home. Whatever your reasons, freelance VO is just about the best job there is. And I can show you how to do it and be successful with my refined and tested 9-step process.

By practicing the practical steps in this book, you'll learn how to make a consistent six-figure income. You don't need expensive studio equipment or a fancy computer. You don't need a background in broadcasting. You don't even need to sound like Casey Kasem!

There's a lot to cover, so if you're ready to get started, just turn the page. And if you're already convinced you'd like extra help to put you over the top, visit www.CanYouDoVO.com to see if VO coaching is right for you.

Ready to get started? Great. Let's do this.

HOW TO READ
THIS BOOK

I've broken down my 9-step VO Blueprint system into three main categories, which are each broken down into three sub-steps. It looks like this:

Get Found

Get Heard

Get Hired

In **Get Found**, you'll first learn how to set up and optimize your recording space. The number one problem I see—or rather, hear—with beginning VO talent is not a problem with their microphone, their recording software or their computer setup. The number one thing affecting your audio quality isn't any of these things. It's your recording space. I'll show you the two keys to a quality recording space, and how to select your ideal recording space for maximum effect.

Next, we'll go over recording equipment. You do not need a $500 microphone and the latest, fastest computer hardware. You also don't need expensive recording software. Here we'll talk about all things microphones, pop filters, headphones, and computers. I'll show you how to get set up quickly and inexpensively, and tell you what equipment you need to buy and what costly gizmos you should avoid. You can get set up with everything you need to succeed even if you're on a budget.

Once you're set up and ready to roll, it's time to create your do-it-yourself (DIY) demo. Your DIY demo is your key to marketing your VO talent and starting to get work. And you can build yours quickly and easily, without hiring an audio coach or expensive producer. I'll show you what to include in your demo, how long it should be, and how to find professional scripts to use.

In **Get Heard**, you'll start on the path to actually getting your DIY demo heard by professional audio producers and getting auditions and work.

You'll start by **Creating Free Accounts** on popular freelance websites. I'll show you why free sites are better when you're just starting out, and how to leverage these sites for success.

We'll also talk about audiobooks, and how to get started recording them if that's your thing. Even if you don't want to do make audiobooks a significant portion of your business, you should do a few of them when you're first getting established because it provides you the opportunity to make some money while you practice and hone your VO and editing techniques.

Once you're on the path to getting paying VO work, I'll show you how to **Track Your Numbers**. VO is a business like any other and should be treated as such. I'll show you exactly what metrics you should keep track of.

Once you've got some paying work under your belt, it's time to **Create a Pro Demo**. With your professional demo, you'll work with an audio producer to create a demo with music and sound effects to really sell your VO talents. With your pro demo in hand you'll be ready to compete on a higher level for national ads and bigger, better paying clients. You'll be ready to create accounts with pay-to-play sites (platforms that provide access to auditions for a fee) and gain a higher level of exposure to lucrative opportunities. Your pro demo is your key to playing with the big boys and girls. I'll walk you through everything you need to create the right pro demo for you.

Finally, in **Get Hired**, I'll show you how to start landing interesting, high-paying assignments from producers all over the planet. We'll **Build Your Marketing Machine**, where I'll show you my winning, time-tested marketing strategies that helped me go from a relative nobody to an experienced VO artist making a multiple six-figure income. You'll learn how to set up multiple marketing channels that keeps landing you work even if one of them dries up. I'll also teach you how to put some of these channels on autopilot so they bring you clients even while you sleep. I'll even show you how to use Google to find more clients than you would ever have time to work with. Once you've located some prospective clients, I'll tell you exactly what to say to them to start building a relationship with them.

Once your marketing machine is in place, it's time to **Perfect Your Technique**. That means both in marketing and performance. I will show you a lot of marketing techniques that have worked for me, but no one can predict which ones will work for you. You might have better luck with cold-calling than paid sites, for example. Perfecting your marketing technique means trying everything, then refining what works best for you. But I will teach you some proven strategies to help you deliver your best performance each and every time. You'll learn simple strategies that will help you deliver the right style and attitude for the piece you're working on as well as connect with the listener.

Perfecting your performance is just as important as solidifying your marketing strategies. It is rare these days in VO to get called into a studio and work with a director, and we lack the objectivity to be honest assessors of our own work.

Finally, you'll round out your skills and get help if you're stuck with some **Personal Coaching**. Everyone, myself included, needs a little help at some point in their career. Personal coaching is here if you need it to give you some feedback and guidance and provide a sounding board if you've plateaued or find yourself backsliding. I'll show you what to look for in a coach, how to get the best results from coaching, and when to walk away from a coach that is not helping you.

This is the only optional step in my 9-step VO Blueprint system. But if my own career is any indicator, you will want to take advantage of coaching at some point, and you'll be glad to have some guidance in this area.

SPECIAL BONUS CHAPTER: AUDIOBOOK NARRATION

Because I want this to be the best book on the planet about how to be a well-paid VO, I've recruited my friend and audiobook narrator extraordinaire Tom Parks to teach you all the ins and out of becoming a successful audiobook narrator. He'll show you the best places to find audiobook narration work and the habits that made him a successful six-figure audiobook narrator.

That's it, your 9-step VO Blueprint system in a nutshell. Now let's get started.

GET FOUND

Set Up Your Recording Space

Throughout my 17 years in VO I have recorded thousands of projects and listened to hundreds of hours of audio from my coaching students. What this experience has taught me is that the number one barrier to success in this business is the quality of your audio.

This may come as no surprise. But what might surprise you is the number one thing that affects your audio quality. It's not your microphone. It's not your editing software. It's not how old your computer is.

No, the number one thing that affects your audio quality the most is your recording space. Your recording space impacts the quality of your audio more than any other factor.

So how do you set up a great recording space? That is the subject of this chapter.

There are two factors that impact the quality of your recording space: quietness and acoustic treatment.

Quietness

There is no such thing as a 100% silent home studio. It doesn't matter how much you've shielded it from the outside world. It doesn't matter what time you record. No space is going to be free from outside ambient noise 100% of the time. It's just not possible.

We all have to deal with noise. For a time I lived in the flight path of a major airport with a neighbor who had his own private shooting range (we lived in a semi-rural area). Everyone, myself included, has to deal with occasional noise. The neighbor's dog. Kids playing down the street. The Amazon Prime van. Construction noise. You name it, we've all had to deal with it at some point during our day. The key is to understand that added noise is unavoidable and plan accordingly.

Here is my two-step process for finding the home recording space that is right for you.

1. Don't make any assumptions. If you're reading this book, you may already have what you think is the perfect space in your home already picked out. Don't go settling in with your microphone and laptop just yet. Check the place out first. Check out every possible recording space in your home.

Pick the time you are most likely going to be able to record and go sit in that space and just listen. You'll be amazed at the things we don't hear when noise doesn't matter, when we let things kind of drone on in the background while we're going about our day. Listen for the stuff you usually tune out, the constant environmental noise you don't hear anymore because you've grown used to it.

You'll not only discover or rediscover these noises, but you'll notice a traffic pattern to these sounds. What time does the mail usually run? When does the morning paper *thwack* against your front door? What time do the neighbor's kids get off the school bus? When are airplanes most likely to fly overhead.

If you're investigating your basement as a possible recording space, what sounds does it make, and when? Does your water heater refill during the time you want to record? Can you hear the house settling? The steady hiss and hum of the air handler? Your family's footsteps on the floor above you?

The family cat, which somehow sounds like a galloping Clydesdale when it's going up and down the stairs?

What about your home office or bedroom? Go there at the time you plan to record and listen to the sounds this room makes.

Thanks to the pandemic, you've probably been in this situation. You're on a Skype or Zoom call and somebody flushes a toilet nearby, or your dog goes nuts. There's few things more embarrassing. Fortunately, most folks are used to this by now, and are pretty understanding. But you'll never live it down if you have sounds like this in your VO recordings.

By now you might be wondering, what makes a good home recording space? Great question!

Typically, the more interior to your house you can get, the better. Rooms with outside walls typically cause problems, and you will hear all kinds of outside noises. My first studio was inside a walk-in closet in our master bedroom. It was far from perfect, but it worked pretty well and blocked a lot of noise. You'd be surprised how well an interior closet full of hanging clothes will block noise and keep your voice from bouncing around, which we'll cover in just a bit.

2. Acoustic Treatment. Now that you've decided on your space, it's time to make sure it is given proper acoustic treatment. Not only do you want to cut down on as much outside noise as possible, you also don't want your voice bouncing off the walls, which will give your recordings an echo effect like you're in a tunnel. Acoustic treatment absorbs the reflection of sound waves bouncing off the walls.

I mentioned closets before, and how hanging clothes make excellent sound absorbers. I bought a cheap mattress cover from Walmart and stapled it to the wall in mine to absorb the sound, and it worked great.

Other cheap, easy acoustic treatments include moving blankets, which you can hang or stack in your space to absorb the sound, and couch cushions. When I'm recording from our vacation home in South Carolina, I use a card table surrounded by couch cushions. Nothing fancy by any stretch of the imagination, but it more than gets the job done.

The key is to be resourceful. Look around your attic or local Goodwill. You can even go professional and use acoustic foam, which comes in easy-to-install panels. The material looks similar in shape to those egg carton mattress toppers, but that is *not* the same stuff. The denser the acoustic foam is, the better. If it's light and airy the sound will pass right through it, and you'll still have that bouncy echo quality to your audio.

Check your noise floor. The noise floor is the noise your room makes when you're not talking. To determine your chosen space's noise floor, go in there with your microphone and recording software and set the gain on your mic so your recorded audio peaks at -3db (decibels). Then, with your mic and recording software turned on, be quiet for several seconds. After 5 to 10 seconds stop the recording and then listen and watch the recording levels. You want your noise floor to be no louder than -60db. Lower is even better. These are negative numbers, so -70db is better than -60db, while at -50db your noise floor is a bit too high.

Keep listening, recording, and checking the audio levels until it sounds just right. If it's still too loud, or there's too much sound reflection (echo) keep adding acoustic treatment and/or other barriers until it's quieter and you stop getting that hollow sound.

Remember, the quality of your recording space is exponentially more important than the quality of your microphone. I started out making $100k a year with a $50 microphone all because I had a quiet space that was well acoustically treated.

Noise Suppression. If you've done all you can do and you're still getting around -50db you can use noise suppression software. The one I recommend is called NS1, and it works great. It's like a Magic Eraser for background noise. It's very affordable (especially when it goes on sale, which it frequently does) and available at Waves.com.

Bass traps. If you have a deep voice or a space that has a lot of bass for some reason, a bass trap will do the trick. These are thicker pieces of acoustic foam or material that come in various shapes and sizes. Many of them are designed to mount in corners, and you can get a pack of them from Amazon inexpensively.

Kaotica Eyeball. This is a big foam ball that fits over your microphone. It basically treats the space immediately around your microphone rather than the walls of your recording space. There are various types that fit almost any microphone. You can check them out, and see if there is a model for your mic, at KaoticaEyeball.com.

Recording on the road? When I was just getting started, one of my first big clients was Rosetta Stone, and I had to go to Virginia for a week to record in their studio, and then record auditions in the evenings from my hotel room. You'd be surprised how much noise suppression you can get just by building a pillow fort around your microphone. You probably won't have to do much in-studio work for clients these days, but a lot of people want to work from the road while traveling full time, living the digital nomad lifestyle. Be creative, but keep it simple. There are still plenty of options available for you if your space is always changing.

What about computer noise? If you've worked on a computer for any length of time, you've noticed that PCs and laptops have fans in them to keep them cool, as well as a hard disk that needs to spin in order for your computer to read and access the data it contains. This can be annoying when you're trying to record. To cut down on this, you could get a computer with an SSD (solid state drive). Some of the newer models are fanless which eliminates a common source of noise. At the time that I'm writing this book, I have a nearly 8-year-old Macbook Pro that I use on the road. It has an SSD and it also uses a fan which can get quite loud at times. To solve this program, I use an external monitor which allows me to keep the computer a distance from me (and usually with pillows or coach cushions between us).

In my studio (which has a nearly 8-year-old iMac) I keep the computer outside of my booth and connected to my recording software and interface with long cables. My booth insulates me from the noisy fan, and all is well.

Pre-Fab Audio Space. Since I just mentioned it, you're probably wondering about my audio booth. A few years into this, after I was making good money, I invested in a Whisper Room. It's a 3 1/2' x 5' booth lined with acoustic foam. They come in a variety of sizes and different levels of sound isolation. It works great, but they are *very* expensive. I do not recommend these if you're just starting out, and you don't need one in order to make a nice six-figure income.

DIY Recording Booth. If you're handy, or know someone who is, you could probably build a great sound-proofed recording booth on your own. I just Googled "recording booth diy" and found a YouTube video that will show you how to build a vocal booth for under a hundred bucks.

Again, you don't have to go to such measures, but if you really don't have a space you can acoustically treat very well this could do the trick.

Visit www.CanYouDoVO.com to see if VO coaching is right for you.

Now that you've got your space as quiet as you can make it, it's time to get your recording equipment, which is the subject of the next chapter.

RECORDING EQUIPMENT

I've already explained how your recording space is the most important factor in the quality of your audio. But you won't have any audio at all without recording equipment. In this chapter, we're going to go over everything you need to put your best professional VO artist self out into the world. Let's do this.

Your Microphone

This is where most people get lost in the weeds. You probably don't have a background in broadcasting and you're not a sound engineer, so you don't know which microphone is best for your purposes. And with the rise and popularity of podcasting, Twitch streaming, and Tiktoking, there are hundreds of different models of mics on the market in every style, color, and price range.

So to cut through the clutter, I'm going to talk about a few basic types of microphones and how well they work for VO.

Condenser microphones. They are typically omnidirectional, meaning they pick up sound from all directions. Condenser mics are one of the most popular mics for studio recording. They are sensitive and pick-up a broad range of audio frequencies.

Dynamic Cardioid microphones. Directional mics, made for broadcast applications.

Shotgun microphones. Very popular, these mics are small, thin and long, which makes them really good directional mics, which makes your voice sound punchy and clear. Also, they don't pick up a lot of extra noise.

USB microphones. A few years ago I would have warned you against using these, but the quality has gotten much better and there are some really good USB mics on the market now. A USB mic is called that because it plugs into your computer via USB cable. USB mics are any microphone with a USB connector, and can be a condenser or other type of mic. Many people prefer these because they plug directly into the PC or laptop and don't require an interface like these other mics do.

The one I used to start out is the Fifine K670, which you can get for around fifty bucks on Amazon. It is a condenser mic. Most anyone (except the best audio engineers) would be able to tell the different between my Fifine and $100 condenser microphone.

Remember, you don't need a $500 or $1000 (or higher) microphone to be successful in this business. I built a six-figure income with a used Marshall MXL microphone that can purchased online for about $50. One of the great things about the VO business is that you don't need to spend a lot of money in order to make a lot of money.

Interface. I mentioned interfaces above, so let's go into more detail on what that means. An interface is just a little box your microphone plugs into, and then plugs into your computer via USB (or any other popular input). The interface turns your analog microphone input into a digital sound file you can manipulate with your computer's recording software.

The interface I use is the Universal Audio Apollo Twin. I also own the Focusrite Scarlett Solo. It's a two-channel interface, which is more than you'll need for VO work. In my opinion, both are excellent interfaces. I would definitely recommend not spending more than $100 or so on your first audio interface.

Computer. I've got some great news for you. You don't have to upgrade your computer hardware to get stared in VO. Whatever system you have right now is perfectly fine. I've recorded VO on both Windows and Mac-based computers, and both work great. As I mentioned earlier, I'm using an 8-year-old iMac and a 2015 Macbook Pro for when I'm traveling. You don't need a lot of processing power or a lot of RAM to do this kind of work.

Noise. We covered this in the previous chapter. Your hard drive is a spinning disk with a fan to keep it cool. That stuff makes noise. The newer SSD drives don't have this problem, but they sometimes make different noises.

To cut down on computer noise, the best strategy is to keep your computer away from your microphone. Mine is 4 or 5 feet away, outside my recording booth. I use a separate screen, mouse, and keyboard connected to it via USB to control my recording software from inside the booth.

Recording Software. Your audio quality is going to be the same no matter what recording software you use. What you pay for with recording software are different feature sets and editing tools. A Mac comes with Garage Band already installed, and will allow you to do everything you need to do in VO. If you have a Windows computer, you can download Audacity for free. It's a fully featured digital audio workstation (DAW), and has everything you need to record studio quality audio.

My favorite recording software is Adobe Audition. It's designed especially for voice recordings and contains about every tool and software plugin that you'll ever need already included.

Programs like Pro Tools and Logic Pro are great, but have way more horsepower and functionality than you need. These programs also have a high learning curve. Hit up YouTube for tutorials if you go this route.

TwistedWave is an audio editor available for Mac and at time of this writing, there's a beta version for Windows. A license key will run you almost $100, and there are subscription plans as well.

Again, you don't need pricey software with a lot of bells and whistles that is time-consuming to learn, especially when you're first starting out. Garage Band and Audacity are free, and will do everything you will ever need them to do.

Headphones. Again, you don't need anything really fancy. The main thing is that need to be able to hear your audio clearly so you can properly edit it. You need something comfortable, with ear material that breathes—you're going to be wearing them in your recording booth for hours at a time—and lets you hear well enough to edit.

I use a pair of Ultrasone HFI 15G headphones. They don't make them anymore, but the Ultrasone brand is still around, and there is probably something similar. They cost me a little over $100. Thanks to the popularity of podcasting and online and PC gaming, there are tons of different headphones on the market that are good quality, comfortable to wear, and relatively inexpensive.

If you're on a budget, you can get a whole lot of mileage in VO out of inexpensive equipment. Remember, if you get your recording space just right, everything else will fall into place.

> If you want to learn more about VO, visit
> www.CanYouDoVO.com to see if VO coaching is
> right for you.

Now that you've got your recording space optimized, and you've purchased your hardware and software, it's time to Get Heard! Read on.

CREATING YOUR DIY DEMO

OK. You've got your recording space set up. You've selected the right microphone. You've got your computer running some great recording software. Now it's time to create your do-it-yourself demo.

But before we dive in, a little background.

Traditional VO wisdom would tell you to first hire a coach and train, then record a professional demo, then get an agent, and then start getting work. It was the advice that I was given when I first started out. Let me just say this, the first agent that signed me (about 16 years) . . . I have NEVER booked a job through them.

All that to say that if you view your agent as your gateway to success . . . good luck!

But times have changed. Today it is entirely possible to get started on a shoestring budget, record professional, world-class audio with inexpensive equipment and free software, and start making money right away with a DIY demo.

Now let's get to it.

Why do you need a demo?

The purpose of a demo is to provide something that your potential clients can hear and get a sense of who you are and what you sound like. The DIY demo is the way you stage yourself, the way you sell yourself. The demo is your sales pitch. Your demo lets the client know what you're capable of.

Your DIY demo should show your capabilities in terms of the breadth and depth of what you're able to do. It shows the client what you sound like when you're excited, concerned, casual, authoritative, happy, sad, low energy, high energy, etc.

Your DIY demo is a "dry" demo, without music or special effects. Just your voice. Unless you're an experienced audio producer, I recommend staying away from the fancy bells and whistles of a pro demo, at least for now. You will create a professional demo eventually, but we'll talk about that in a later chapter. For now, stick with the basic, bare bones, dry voice DIY demo.

What Kind of DIY Demo?

By now you're probably wondering what kind of samples to create for your demo. While you can always specialize and create a different sort of demo later, I recommend starting out with a commercial demo.

A commercial demo has samples of commercial work. This is mission critical, regardless of what kind of VO work you are looking for. Between 75% and 80% of my work is corporate work—explainer videos, on-hold messages and the like—but my clients hired me based on my commercial demo.

How many commercials? I recommend doing 4-6 scripts for your demo. Feel free to do more than 6 if you'd like, but I wouldn't do less than 4.

Where do you get scripts? That's the easy part. You get scripts for your DIY demo by transcribing actual commercials. Don't worry. I've never heard of anyone getting in trouble for using a portion of a commercial script for demo purposes. As long as you're not profiting off of some else's material it's considered fair use.

The easiest source for commercials is YouTube or ISpot.tv. ISpot.tv will even let you browse commercials by industry, most seen, and top ad spend (ISpot.tv/browse). You'll have access to virtually every television commercial ever made. Just watch, listen, and transcribe.

Choosing from thousands of commercials may sound overwhelming, but don't worry. You don't need to use more than 10-15 seconds of each commercial. Transcribe them, record them individually, and put them together into one audio file when you're done. *Voila*, you have your DIY demo.

Select commercials based on the emotions they evoke. Listen to the original speaker to see what was required of them when they were producing it. Use samples that are upbeat, high energy, and happy along with samples that are more somber or serious. An announcement for the upcoming monster truck rally is more upbeat than an ad for a funeral home. A giant closeout sale has more positive vibes than an ad for a cancer treatment center. You get the idea.

You're trying to elicit an emotional response, make the listener feel something. We'll cover this in greater detail in a later chapter.

Once you have your script samples, edit them together into one audio file. WAV format is best, but an mp3 is much smaller, which allows you to easily email it to potential clients and share online. When in doubt, create both. That way your prospects can get whatever format they're most comfortable with.

Now that your DIY demo is done, it's time to send it out, sit back, and let the clients roll in, right?

Sorry, no. I hate to burst your bubble, but you're not quite ready just yet. You should send it out to potential clients, but while you're waiting, you still need to work on perfecting your demo.

Rerecord your demo at least once a week for 6-8 weeks. Why? Because when you're first getting started in this business you're going to improve very quickly. As you get better, you want to make sure you are constantly presenting your best work. You will always be in the process of getting better, but there's no reason to wait until you think you're good enough. You can start making money right now even as you improve.

Make sure each iteration of your DIY demo has a broad variety of styles and different textures of your personality. Remember, you want to come off as serious, authoritative, light-hearted, etc.

Another often-overlooked aspect of your DIY demo is your audio editing. Not only will you need to edit your demo, you will also have to edit the VOs you send to clients.

It takes a while to develop your editing skills, so it's expected that the editing on your first demo isn't going to be all that great. But as you rerecord your demo, your editing will get better along with your VO narration work.

By now you're probably wondering, "Can I actually make money with a dry, voice over, DIY demo?"

The answer is a resounding yes! In fact, I guarantee you can make a six-figure income with a DIY demo. I've done it, and my students have done it.

Think of your DIY demo as a proof of concept. If you can't make money with that, you probably can't make money with a pro demo. And at least you didn't spend thousands of dollars on a pro demo in order to find out.

> If you want to learn more about VO, visit www.CanYouDoVO.com to see if VO coaching is right for you.

Now that you've got your DIY demo ready to go, it's time to **GET HEARD!**

GET HEARD

Create Free Accounts

I've talked at length about how, in the olden days of VO, you had to have a professional demo and an agent before you could even hope to get any work.

Fortunately, those days are gone. You can start doing VO with very little investment. Over the years I've found that just throwing money into stuff doesn't automatically make it work.

Most of what you need in VO, including your marketing, doesn't take much money to get it going.

In order to be successful in VO you need to put yourself where your clients are. You want to get your DIY demo into as many ears as possible, as efficiently as possible, and at the lowest cost.

So what does that mean?

That means setting up free accounts on freelance websites. Generally speaking, at the time of the writing of this book, the following sites are some of the best places to get started.

Fiverr.com

Fiverr is an online platform where people can get all kinds of services, from book writing to cover design to custom spreadsheets, starting at just five bucks. But don't worry, there are all kinds of add-ons and upsells Fiverr creators employ to make more money. In VO, you can deliver a higher quality file, faster turnaround, commercial usage, or broadcast usage for a higher fee. But don't focus on the money right now. Focus on delivering a quality product.

Fiverr favors buyers of freelance services over the service providers. That means in order to show up in Fiverr's search results you need to deliver a quality product on time. Once you start getting positive customer ratings and good reviews, Fiverr will show your profile to more and more people looking for VO narration.

You won't make much on the platform in the beginning, but that's OK. These types of jobs won't take you very long to do, you'll get great practice with voice narration and using your recording software, and over time these small jobs will add up to big money.

One year I made $24,000 on Fiverr. I also made $5,000 on a single job, so the money is there. You just have to be patient and work the system.

I'm no Fiverr expert by any stretch of the imagination. But I know someone who is. My daughter.

Mallory started out as my assistant 12-13 years ago. Today she is a stay-at-home mom making six figures on Fiverr working just 20 hours a week. She has even created a training course on how to use the platform to get VO work. You can check it out at MalloryFiverrTraining.com.

While I'm not Fiverr expert (like my daughter), I can share with you the basics.

Set up a free account on Fiverr.

Upload your DIY demo.

Search for other VO talent to see what verbiage they're using. How do they market themselves on the platform? On Fiverr, what is their starting rate? What are their upsells?

Understand that it will take some time to gain any traction. Part of being a success on Fiverr is being on the platform for a while. Fiverr makes you earn their trust. You have to deliver great work that gets 5-star reviews. Do that enough and Fiverr will direct more traffic to your gig. Just be patient and do outstanding work on every job that comes your way. And remember, it's great practice and you won't have to do any auditions to get work on the platform.

Upwork.com

I'm not on Upwork myself, but I have a number of students who are doing quite well on there. I encourage you to upload your demo there and play around with the platform.

Voicebunny.com

Owned by pay to play site Voice123.com, Voicebunny is free. It is set up a bit differently. Everything happens fast on Voicebunny. The people who succeed there are those who are available to respond quickly to jobs.

That may not work for you, and that's fine. Some people are sitting in front of their computer all day, waiting on gigs. You may not be able to do that. If you can't do a job right then, don't worry about it. You'll get the next one.

But the thing I like the most about Voicebunny is that if you're invited to audition you get paid, and if you win the audition and get the gig, you get paid more.

A couple of caveats. There is a barrier to entry on Voicebunny. You have to apply to be included on the website, and you have to pass a two-part test.

The first test is of your audio quality. Don't worry if you don't pass this part. They will give you suggestions for improvement, and you can submit again. If you follow their suggestions, you'll get your audio approved.

The second test is an audition. The audition is more about your ability to follow direction and respond quickly, within a 4-5 hour window.

Voicebunny is a very viable option. I have students who make really good money using the platform.

ACX

ACX stands for Audiobook Creation Exchange. Owned by Amazon, it is the go-to site for audiobook narration. Creating a profile and uploading your demo to ACX will get you access to thousands of auditions from hundreds of audiobook producers and publishers.

Even if you don't plan on doing audiobooks exclusively, it's helpful for your career to get some audiobook narration under your belt. You'll get tons of practice using your editing software, the pay can be pretty decent—around $50-$100 per finished hour on the low end—and you can do these when you're in between other VO projects. In my early days, I always had an audiobook assignment going while awaiting a commercial or corporate narration gig.

ACX will even let you search for gigs by pay rate.

Royalty Share. Some books on ACX pay a royalty share. These assignments are usually from independent authors who either don't have the big bucks up front to shell out for audiobook narration or don't expect to sell that many books.

But that may not necessarily be the case. If someone offers you a royalty share, look up the title in print and eBook on Amazon, if those versions have already been published. If the book in the top of its category, especially a broad category like Science Fiction, it's probably selling really well, and will probably do just as well in audiobook format.

My point is don't discount royalty share deals altogether. These deals pay you for seven years, and you get editing, recording, and narrating experience that will pay you huge dividends later in the form of better-paying gigs.

If you want to record audiobooks, create a specialized DIY demo containing three 30-second segments from three different books in three different genres that you find interesting. You don't need "special" scripts for audiobook narration. Simply find some books you like (you may already own them or can probably find them online) select about 30 seconds worth of the script and start recording.

The audiobook market isn't quite as competitive as the commercial market. You can even reach out to audiobook publishers directly and create a relationship with them.

Full confession time. In my entire VO career, I've only narrated 41 audiobooks. I don't do it anymore because I make more money in the long term doing shorter commercial and corporate narration work.

But I know that some of you will want to do audiobook narration full-time, and because I want this to be the best book on VO you'll ever pick up, I've teamed up with a buddy of mine who makes six figures a year doing audiobook narration exclusively. And he's going to tell you everything you need to know about getting audiobook narration work in a special bonus chapter at the end of this book.

There's one more free site you should sign up for. Soundcloud will allow you to upload your demo so you can share it with producers. People are squeamish about receiving email attachments, so just send them the Soundcloud link to your demo (if you don't have a website yet) instead. It makes your marketing that much faster.

These sites are all free, you can get going with just a DIY demo, and you can start immediately.

> Visit www.CanYouDoVO.com to see if VO coaching is right for you.

Now that you've set up profiles on these free sites, it's time to get down to the business of treating VO like a business. That means tracking your numbers.

TRACK YOUR NUMBERS

What I'm about to reveal to you in this step will separate you, the serious VO artist who wants to make this a viable business, from the thousands of part-time hobbyists.

I firmly believe that to be truly successful in voice-over you have to treat it like a business. There is simply no other way.

This is the point where a lot of VO narrators drop the ball. They only focus on the performance side of the business. I know a number of people who are world class talent, yet only work a few times a year. That's not a career. That's a side hustle. That's a hobby.

I don't want that for you, and since you're reading this book, I don't think you do either. I want you to make VO a raging full-time success, where you're booked solid with work on a consistent basis.

Here's how to do that.

One of the biggest things you need to do in order to treat your VO business like a business instead of a side hustle is to keep track of your numbers.

Now before you run away screaming, I'm not talking about graphs and pie charts, or spreadsheets and P&L statements here. You do not need an MBA, nor do you need to track every conceivable analytic in order to do this. But there are a few things that are essential for you to know.

And here they are:

When I first got started doing VO, the primary thing I wanted to know was how much money I made per day. Now, in my situation, I had been downsized and had all day to do VO work. So what did I need to generate on the daily to pay my bills and feed my family? In other words, what did I need to survive?

That number, for me, was $200. I knew that if I could make that number per day, on average, I could survive on voice-over work alone.

Your number might be different. You have a different lifestyle and live in a different area of the country where the cost of living is higher or lower than mine. Use your current day job to establish a baseline. Just multiply your hourly rate by 8 hours to get how much you make per day at your job. You can also add up your monthly expenses and divide by 30. This would give you a number you can attempt to work toward.

What did this look like for me and my VO business? Early on I was doing a lot of small market radio and TV ads for $50 (or less) per spot. These were smaller projects. So in order to hit my $200 per day I needed to do multiple jobs each day to survive. Or sometimes, it was one explainer video for $200. You see what I mean.

Now that I knew how many and what type of jobs to get in order to hit that $200 a day threshold, I then needed to figure out what I had to do in order to get those jobs.

So, for example, if I know it takes 100 auditions per week to get one $200 job then that's what I had to do. I then broke that down even further. 100 auditions per week comes out to 20 auditions per day Monday through Friday.

It might take you more. It might take you less. You don't really know until you actually do the marketing and keep track of your results. Keep track of how many emails you send out versus how many responses you get. Keep track of how many producers listening to your demo leads to one audition.

This means that you must also track your marketing. For example, I do a lot of direct marketing. I know that I have to send at least 100 emails in order to get one response. Now that doesn't mean they'll hire me. It just means they're now a warm lead who may need my services at some point later on down the road.

Of those responses, I need 5-6 positive responses to get one job, and each job these days pays an average of $400.

That means that if I want one new client a week I need to send 400-500 emails or phone calls per day. That may sound daunting, but if that's the number I need to hit in order to grow my business, then that's what I'm going to do.

Know what your clients are worth. Let's say my average client is worth $5000 in revenue per year. If I want to make $50,000 per year then I know I need at least 10 clients paying me that much per year each. I also know how many jobs I need to do and how many emails to send out to get those jobs. *And*

I know what marketing channels got me that $5,000 client. It's all interconnected.

The better all that gets, the better your batting average. It takes work to get up to that level, but it can be done. I'm living proof.

Keep track of your daily and weekly numbers to identify trends. All businesses have an ebb and flow to them, even VO. I've been in situations where it seemed like a slow week, but by looking at my numbers I could see, for example, the second week in June is always slow, and I can adjust accordingly.

Keeping track of trends allows you to adjust your numbers or just plan for a dip in revenue. By knowing the peaks and valleys you can better plan ahead, as well as identify times when you're going to be busier than usual and prepare for them.

Keep track of your highest producing clients. One of the biggest goals of your business is not to simply stay afloat but to grow. And not all clients are created equal.

I keep a list of which of my clients produced the most revenue ranked from most to least. This gives me a keen insight. Your biggest revenue producers aren't always the folks for which you worked the hardest. Busyness doesn't always equate to profitability.

Now, let's put all these metrics together. If you know what marketing channels make you the most money, and which of your clients produce the most revenue for you, then this tells you which marketing channels and clients to let go.

Wait a minute, Bill. You want me to let clients *go*?

Yes. If they aren't serving you or your business. Let me ask you a question: are you going to keep trying to accommodate everybody, or let the least producing ones go in order to make room for higher producing clients?

By the same token, are you going to keep marketing streams going that aren't bringing you high-paying clients? Or are you going to drop those and add more streams that get you better results?

Understand your numbers. Know what you need to make per year, how many clients/assignments you need to make that amount, your most productive marketing channels and the lifetime revenue each VO client is worth. You'll be able to navigate slow patches and grow your business a lot faster.

If you're still unclear on whether or not VO is right for you, visit www.CanYouDoVO.com to see if VO coaching is right for you.

Now let's move onto the next step: Creating Your Professional Demo!

CREATE YOUR
PRO DEMO

How times have changed.

Just five short years ago I would have told you to not even think about doing VO work until you had a professional demo. And once you did, you'd be competing right out of the gate with a much higher level of competition. In today's world, this is thankfully no longer the case.

I've showed you how to get started with a do-it-yourself demo and how to use it to start getting work—and start getting paid. And you should already be doing that.

But there will come a time when your DIY demo is no longer enough, and you will need a pro demo to take the next step.

But when is this time? Is it a certain date on a calendar? How can you tell when it's time for you to create a professional demo?

When Do You Need A Pro Demo?

My rule of thumb is that you should have a pro demo produced when you have made enough at VO to pay for it. It's really that simple.

A good pro demo is going to cost you several thousand dollars. At this time I'm writing this boo, I charge $2500 to produce a pro demo. I'm priced higher than some, lower than others (but the product is always very competitive.). This is not a pitch for production services but rather to make you aware of the costs involved.

If you've done enough VO work to pay for a pro demo, you can get one produced without going into the red.

What does a pro demo get you?

A pro demo does one thing very well. It creates opportunities for you. It also attracts attention, stages you, and makes you look and sound like a viable candidate for a job, which usually comes in the form of an audition.

Your pro demo isn't a guarantee that you'll get work, but it opens doors for you and makes you look and sound like an experienced professional.

A pro demo is mission critical in order to progress up the ladder of voice over sucess.

Your pro demo must be a high-quality product. Better performance, better production values, music, mixing, and audio quality. It should sound like it was pulled right off of network television.

Your pro demo allows you to compete at a higher level for better, higher paying jobs.

What type of demo should you do?

One mistake I see people make is doing is initially spreading themselves too thin by getting a demo produced in every niche they may be interested in. So what type of demo should you get produced?

I recommend that everyone start with a commercial demo. No matter what type of VO work you end up doing, you need a commercial demo. I do primarily corporate work as well as commercial promo work. And I got all of it off the strength of my pro demo.

Stay away from niche demos at first. It will take a while to determine what niche(s) the market thinks you're best at. Don't worry about an e-learning demo if you're planning to focus on the e-learning niche. At least when you're first starting out. If you're marketing yourself well that commercial demo will show you in your best light in every facet of VO.

What Your Pro Demo Should Look and Sound Like

Your pro commercial demo should be around 60 seconds. I've even seen some 30-second demos, but I'm not a huge fan. Maybe one day attention spans will have shortened to the point that 30-and maybe even 20-second demos will be in fashion. But I'm not convinced that we're there . . . yet. Audio producers and agents are used to hearing 60-second demos. Give them what they expect.

So, what goes into that 60 seconds? You need to have 5-10 seconds each of 7-8 different commercials. Don't worry, your pro demo producer will select these scripts for you. They will also mix in the appropriate music and sound effects, making you sound like you came right off of television or radio.

Your pro demo should show a range of your capabilities and different aspects of your personality. Remember, people respond more to personality, point of view, and emotion than style.

Each script should give listeners a different aspect or slice of your personality. Again, don't worry too much about this. The producer is going to direct you and get a read from you that you wouldn't be able to get from yourself. You don't have the objectivity to do it well. None of us do.

Selecting a Pro Demo Producer

Pro demos are pricey, and rates vary widely. Get several quotes, but don't make your final decision based solely on price. At the end of the day, make sure you get exactly what you want (and what will best help you get work). A finished product that will showcase you, make you sound like you were pulled right off network TV. Something that shows you and what you can do in the best possible light.

Ask for samples of the producer's work. Make sure they are someone you can work with. Someone who's work you respect. Make sure you get along with them. You don't want to have a personality clash with your producer.

If you can't afford the producer you want, wait until you can. Do a few more VO jobs and save up that money. The money you spend on a pro demo can be made back in short order, so you're better off waiting until you've got the money to do the best pro demo you can possibly produce.

Still have a question on the ins and outs of producing a pro demo? Visit www.CanYouDoVO.com to see if VO coaching is right for you.

All right. Now that you have your pro demo, it's time to **Get Hired!**

GET HIRED

Build Your Marketing Machine

Marketing.

It's a dirty word to many, and the mere mention of it fills them with dread, conjuring images of spreadsheets and complex keyword analytics.

When I first started in freelance VO, the biggest mistake I made was thinking this business was somehow fundamentally different from every other industry on the planet, including those in which I had actually worked.

Following my career in radio, I worked in marketing, and was a later a marketing consultant. I had a background in business, but (based on the advice I heard from VO "experts) figured that what I knew didn't apply to VO. Boy was I wrong, and it showed in my early business in the form of struggling to find enough good-paying clients to sustain me and my family.

Then I started doing what I do best: getting in front of people and staying in front of them, which, when you boil it down to its bare essentials, is all marketing really is. And that's when I started finding success.

Here's how it went down.

One of my earliest clients was Rosetta Stone. I found my VO job with them through Monster.com of all places. I don't even know if Monster is still a thing, but I tried it out, almost on a lark, and found a client.

I spent a week in Virginia with them recording in their studio. I also hauled my computer and recording equipment with me so I could continue recording auditions and projects in my hotel room at night after working at Rosetta Stone all day.

Doing that takes drive and hustle, but it can be done. It takes trying a little bit of everything, but it leads to success.

Remember, your end goal is that you want as many people to hear you as possible. And you must do everything you can to make that happen.

The Marketing Wheel

Think of your marketing strategy as a wheel. Each of your marketing channels is a spoke in that wheel. Marketing isn't a one-size-fits-all approach where you can do one thing, and one thing only, and expect to get endless clients forever and ever.

It's more like a mutual fund portfolio, where you have a bunch of stocks. If one stock doesn't perform well, you still have the others to fall back on.

The same is true with marketing. If one marketing channel dries up, you still have others in place that bring you clients. The more of these channels you have in place, the more stable you are and the more money you make.

Eventually one of these marketing channels may dry up, or cease to be as effective as it once was. Nothing lasts forever. Especially in the VO business.

Occasionally a client will want a different voice. A few years back I was hired by a casino client, and I became the voice for their TV and radio commercials for a couple of years. It was steady, reliable work and I made a lot of money. It was weekly and fun, and I enjoyed it a lot.

Then one day I got a call from the engineer, who told me the casino company came under new management and they wanted to go with a different voice.

Another example is a client that is a big health care system in the state of Michigan. I made many thousands of dollars working for them over the course of several years. It dawned on me one day that it had been several months since I had heard from. It's now been several years without a word. When one of my clients gets a new manager or project lead, it's not unusual for them to hire a new voice. It's simply the nature of the business. Don't expect a call to inform you of the change, because often, you won't.

It's nothing personal, and there are no hard feelings. It's just the culture of the VO business. And in the casino's case, I was happy to get a call from the engineer, who only did so because he liked me. It's rare to even get a phone call to say they're going in a different direction. Clients will just suddenly drop you without warning.

Now, if those were my only two clients, I'd be dead in the water. But because I work hard to actively cultivate multiple marketing channels, I always have work in the pipeline when one of my income streams dries up.

Your Marketing Channels

With all this talk about marketing channels, which ones are best for your VO business?

As I said earlier, this isn't like the old days where you had to have an agent and a pro demo before you even had the slightest chance of getting client work. These days, thanks to the Internet, you've got the entire VO world literally right at your fingertips.

These days, when it comes to marketing you're limited only by your imagination and willingness to put in the work.

Once You Have a Pro Demo

We've covered what to do to get established. Now let's discuss what you should do once you have your pro demo in hand.

After You've Recorded a DIY Demo

Now you're ready to get to the work of building a voice over business! With your DIY demos in hand (commercial and audiobook), you are ready to find some clients!

Websites

Following are the websites I would recommend to set up an account and post your demo(s)

- ACX.com
- Fiverr.com
- Upwork.com
- Thumbtack.com
- VoiceBunny.com
- FindAwayTalent.com
- AhabTalent.com

Once You Have Your Pro Demo

We've covered what to do to get established. Now let's discuss what you should do once you have your pro demo in hand.

Talent Rosters

I don't check job-related websites anymore because I've developed other marketing channels and cultivated direct relationships with clients. Don't worry, you will too.

But if I was just getting started today I absolutely would try to get listed on as many VO talent rosters as possible.

What's a talent roster?

Jump on Google and search "voice talent roster" and you'll find pages and pages of production companies that do nothing but audio production for TV and radio. A couple of big ones are VoiceJockeys.com and VoiceTalentOnline.com.

Potential clients search these sites for the VO talent they want, searching by gender, age range, language spoken, and so on. All of them have a place where you can enter your personal info and upload your demo to be considered for inclusion in the roster.

The great thing about talent rosters is that they do all of your advertising for you. Why email or call TV and radio stations one-by-one when you can get on a handful of rosters that will show you off to their clients?

The downside is these aren't the best paying gigs. You might make $40 for a radio commercial, or $150 for a short TV spot (give or take). On the upside it can become high volume. When I was just starting out I would do 5-6 of these projects per day. Once you have the hang of your recording software, and experience recording scripts, it doesn't take long to create a 30-second commercial. I was cranking out that stuff all day. And just imagine how good you'll get not only at narration but handling your editing software by doing a bunch of these?

Another caveat, you do have to wait for a spot on the roster, and some clients may hire you right away, while others you'll never hear from. That's just the nature of the game.

Pay to Play Sites

Once you've got some VO experience and a quality pro demo, you can try the pay to play sites. I call them pay to play because they charge you a monthly fee for being listed on them.

The two biggest are the aforementioned Voices123 and Voices.com.

These can be a lot of work, involving cattle-call auditions, but they're a great way to develop your talent and abilities and get access to some great-paying work. Not long ago I completed a $12,000 job for client that found me on Voice123.com.

I'll include a third site here as an honorable mention. TheVoiceRealm.com is a bit smaller than Voices123 and Voices.com, but it's a good place to land work.

Pay to play sites are deeper waters, filled with a higher caliber of clients who can typically pay more than those you would have access to on Fiverr or one of the talent rosters. Once you've developed your skills and gained more experience, you'll be ready to swim in these waters.

If you've set up a strong profile and have a good quality demo uploaded, clients will come to you. The casino company found me on a pay to play site, as did the large health care system I mentioned a little earlier.

Direct Marketing

Another scary term, but it doesn't have to be. All it means is that you are reaching out to folks directly. But who?

Video Production Companies

So who should you contact? For VO, that means video production companies. A quick Google search will give you thousands, both large and small, to choose from, many of which use VO talent. To narrow things down a bit, you can search by region.

Once you've located a few you want to contact, call them up and say, "Hi, I'm (your name) and I was hoping I could speak to the person in charge of hiring VO talent."

When you get them on the line, say, "Hi, my name is (your name), and I was calling to see if you're currently accepting VO demos."

Nine times out of ten they'll say "yes." Just ask them what email to send it to, thank them, and hang up. Then send them your demo. If you have a website simply email them a link to it.

This is what marketers call prospecting. They may not be hiring right away, but you'll get on their radar. Remember, the goal here isn't to get a VO job immediately with one phone call. The goal is to get your demo in the hands of someone who can hire you. Even if that ends up being later on down the road.

If you don't want to talk to them on the phone, you can email them instead. People don't like getting unsolicited email attachments because of computer virus fears, so ask for permission before you send your demo. And when you send your demo, send the most recent one you created.

If you can do these things consistently, you're going to be given opportunities. It's just a fact.

YouTube Producers

These days, YouTube is big business, with thousands of video producers using the platform. And they often need VO talent for intros, outros, and ads. A lot of them use Voices.com and Voices123 to find talent, but there's no reason you couldn't contact a few of them directly, bypassing a few gatekeepers and building relationships.

Getting Your Mind Right

Your mindset is an important factor in your success, especially at this stage. Make a game of it. Set a goal to reach out to ten prospects per day, and then work to make that happen. Ten per day is 50 per 5-day workweek. Don't even focus on getting work. Make it all about making as many contacts as you can. With a pace like that it won't be long at all before you start getting work.

Marketing is a funny, fickle beast. You'll find that cold-calling a few video production companies will kick-start one of your other marketing channels. You'll email a couple of demos, and suddenly get a message from a prospective client on Fiverr, or Voices123. I don't know why it happens that way, but it does.

Keeping multiple marketing channels open and working for you is the key to success in this and any business.

Are you still wondering if VO is right for you? Have some questions? Visit www.CanYouDoVO.com to see if VO coaching is right for you.

Now that you've built your marketing machine, it's time to **Perfect Your Technique**.

PERFECT YOUR TECHNIQUE

Now we come to the ninth step in my VO Blueprint system: Perfecting your technique. But what does that mean exactly?

Perfecting your technique is about perfecting your marketing as well as perfecting your performance.

Perfecting Your Marketing

How do you perfect your marketing?

Practice.

I found over time that a number of the marketing spokes I discussed in the previous chapter didn't produce much if anything for me, while a small handful produced a lot. And quite a few of them made up the bulk of my income.

The same will be the case for you. A number of your marketing streams won't produce much, while others will get you the bulk of your clients. In the beginning we have no idea which is which. You will just have to try as many as you can. What works for me may not work as well for you and vice versa. I had a lot of luck in the beginning finding work on Craigslist, of all places. My daughter makes more on Fiverr than I do. Some people get a lot more results with direct marketing. Don't be afraid to try everything. The only way to find out if something works for you or not is to try it.

The worst thing that can happen is that it doesn't work. But with a little patience and time, you will get results.

Keep going. Keep trying new things. Keep practicing and perfecting your marketing techniques.

Perfecting Your Performance

Performance is a challenge for anyone who works alone in a home studio, which is about 99% of us who work in VO. So, when you get frustrated, just know that you are not alone. Most of us work this way and encounter the same problems, the same difficulties and frustrations.

Working in a studio with a director is the exception, not the norm. Most of us go it alone, which means we don't have the feedback we might want or need. We can't hear ourselves the way a director would. We lack the objectivity. Directing yourself would be like trying to be your own therapist.

So how do we perfect our performance? You must figure out as best you can how to deliver your best performance on your own. But how do we do that?

First off, you must remember that it's less about performing and more about communicating.

Let's examine the word performing.

When I think of performing I'm thinking of the theatrical meaning of the word. That's because VO is very different from other modes of performance. The VO medium is very intimate. It's not someone performing on a stage one night for thousands. It's someone communicating with one individual at a time, even though your commercial, corporate training narration, or audiobook might be heard by thousands of people over a much longer period of time.

You aren't performing in the traditional theatrical sense. You are communicating and connecting with people individually.

The ultimate goal in VO—whether you're recording an audition or an actual project—is for the listener to believe you.

Back when I worked in radio, the biggest challenge for on-air talent was to make sure that our audience didn't keep turning the dial when they landed on our station. Or leave as soon as they heard our voice.

Audiences leave because your words aren't resonating with them. They're not connecting with what you're saying because they don't *believe* you.

So how do you get a listener to believe you?

For someone to believe you they have to *feel* what you're saying. When something you hear makes you laugh, makes you afraid, makes you excited, it's because what the speaker said resonated with you, made you stop to lean in really listen to what they were saying.

That's what you want to do. Make them lean in and pay attention. Whether it's an audio producer listening to your demo or audition, the end client, or the end listener. You want whoever is listening to stop and feel something.

Right now, you're probably saying, "Yeah, Bill, that sounds great. But how do we do that?"

For the listener to feel something, you have to feel it first.

That's the rub in VO performance. You have to feel the emotion that you want the listener to feel, be it a casting agent, producer, or the end listener.

But how does that work? How do you conjure up some sort of emotion so that you can feel what you are reading?

Here are a few tips I employ. A few of them will sound a little silly to you. But trust me. They work, and I have used them to book a ton of VO assignments.

Make the script personal. When reading a script, draw from your own experience so that you can feel what you are talking about.

This can be done even if the script is about something you have no prior experience with.

For example, let's say I'm doing a beer ad. I hate beer. I just don't like the taste. Drinking beer has never been something I've enjoyed. But if that's what's on my mind while I'm recording a beer commercial, even at a subconscious level, that's what the audience will hear. If it's not appealing to me it's not going to be appealing to them. The ad won't sell any beer, and I'll probably never get work from that client again.

So instead I have to think of something I love. I love Coke Zero. I drink it every day and always keep plenty of it on hand in the fridge. So in my mind, while I'm recording that beer commercial, I'm going to think about how relaxing and refreshing it is when I pop the tab on ice-cold can of Coke Zero. I have to look at the script and identify with it. I have to ask myself, "If this was me, how would I feel?"

I'll give you another, more concrete, example. I do a lot of hospital VO for clients all over the country. These are very serious, somber ads. So when I'm doing scripts about compassion and care I think about the times when I've visited loved ones in the hospital and remember how I felt.

I think about being in the hospital with my dad when he was dying from cancer, or, when the required tone is a bit lighter, when my kids have been in the hospital for various cuts and scrapes that needed stitches. I feel the compassion, the love, and the concern when I'm reading.

These emotions are carried by the words and will resonate with the listener. They'll believe the words I'm saying. It will feel authentic and genuine.

So, how do you feel about your next script? Or your first?

Err on the side of over-emoting. You can never sound too good. In fact, sometimes if you're a little too perfect it makes you sound less believable. Go for over-feeling a script as opposed to striving to be physically perfect.

Think of some of the commercials or radio ads you've heard over the years. Most of them are at least a little over the top. They're really upbeat, hyper, or bombastic. Or they're super serious, somber, or sad. That hyper emotion is what you're going for when you read a script.

Think about the emotion you want to evoke and then read. People want perceived honesty. If you can do this, you'll be able to book a ton of work.

Use a springboard. Fair warning. This will sound silly to you as you read this, and you'll feel even sillier when you do it. But trust me. It works.

What's a springboard? A springboard is just something you say or do before you record a script that puts you in that scenario.

Don't think of the script as the beginning of what's happening. It needs to feel like a continuation of something that came before, a reaction or response to something that happened "off screen."

A simple word will do the trick. I like to use the word *Hey* as in "Hey, this week at Kroger…" That way you're already in the conversation before it gets started.

You can also say someone's name followed by the script. "Joe, this weekend at Indianapolis Motor Speedway…" This does two things. It keeps it from sounding like a false start and therefore more genuine, and it helps you create the feeling that you are talking one-on-one to a close personal friend.

Another thing you can do is laugh out loud—if appropriate— before reading the script. But only use this trick for something upbeat, not a funeral home or hospital cancer center ad.

Your springboard doesn't have to be verbal. You can try smiling (listeners can hear this in your voice) or moving your hands. Anything that takes you out of your head and into your heart, where people hire you.

And it should go without saying, but you then remove these verbal springboards during the editing process. Only what's actually in the script stays.

If you tend to over project everything, try cutting your volume in half. You can also scream or yell before reading a script. This technique takes you out of your head. If it helps you, "let go" of trying to control the read and simply communicate. A word of caution though . . . be careful not to strain your vocal cords or damage your voice.

I know this sounds bizarre but these springboard techniques have served me well and allowed me to get more jobs and make more money than I would have otherwise.

If you talk too fast—don't worry, most people do—try slowing your cadence. I use my hand as a Metronome, moving it up and down at a slower tempo to force voice to do the same. You can also practice talking so slow that it becomes extremely uncomfortable to do so. Then when you talk normally you'll go slower just because you've over-trained.

Warm-up exercises?

I don't have anything in particular. Sometimes I'll sing or speak a scale up and down. Mostly though I just start with the easiest script of the day, which is usually an e-learning script. That will loosen me up so that I am able to do more demanding scripts later in the day.

Should you take an acting or improv class?

I never have, but I have known folks who did, and they swear by them. Whatever it takes to get you in touch with your emotions and loosen you up. Such activities would also get you out of the house some and interacting, and networking, with other folks, and that's never a bad thing.

Once you *become* a VO artist, the trick becomes *staying* one. By perfecting your technique—both in marketing and the practice of VO itself—you'll be able to remain in this business and make a wonderful living over the long haul.

And if you're still wondering whether or not you have what it takes to succeed in this business, visit www.CanYouDoVO.com to see if VO coaching is right for you.

You've made it! You've gotten through 8 steps in my 9-step system. There's just one final step to take. Are you ready? Then read on as we look at getting personal coaching.

GET PERSONAL COACHING

Let's face it. No one is good at everything.

There will be aspects of your business at which you absolutely excel, while other areas you may find a challenge.

For this reason, we should all be looking for people with more experience and more understanding in whatever field of endeavor we're striving toward.

When I got started in the VO business years ago, a coach told me to do a pro demo and get a talent agent. I did the demo, which cost me a pretty penny, and got several agents. But it simply didn't lead to enough work.

I talked about this earlier in the book, but back in those days, most of the work was obtained through talent agents. The problem and the challenge with that is that you were always competing with an experienced, high-level talent pool for a very small number of jobs. This made it very difficult to get work.

Today is a completely different ballgame. Today, that advice is extremely outdated and no longer relevant. These days less than 2% of my annual income comes through agents, and I have a lot of agents scattered all around the world. If you are only using agencies to get work you're missing out.

Getting a VO job through an agency is like winning the lottery. I'm happy for the people who win, but making that you're sole marketing channel is a terrible business plan.

You need to land jobs on a consistent basis. That means you need to search for other ways to get work.

So, what does this have to do with coaching?

You don't have to wait until you're a top-tier talent with a professional demo. And you don't have to already be at a high level before you can start working with a coach.

Some of these jobs might not pay top dollar but they are eagerly hiring less experienced talent. And every job you take gives you the experience, references, and connections you need to get the next job. And the next...

Coaching Horror Stories

I hear stories quite often from people who have worked with a coach for years who continually tells them they aren't ready to record a demo. That is ridiculous!

If you have a long-time coach who has been telling you to wait . . . and then wait some more, I want you to do one thing right now. I mean right this very minute.

Fire that coach.

You don't have to wait years until you meet someone's arbitrary standard of "good enough." You can start making money right now, learning as you go.

A couple of years ago I was contacted by a well-known actor and VO artist in LA. He wanted to expand his marketing outside of the traditional agency and union business model.

We had a 30-minute phone session where I shared some marketing strategies. After that I didn't hear much from him for the next year, when he booked another session just to thank me for helping him double his income.

I tell you this anecdote not to brag about what a great coach I am, but to show you that you don't need to be dependent upon a coach for every nut and bolt in your business. Do what they say until it doesn't work any longer. Then get some more help.

When do you need a coach?

In my view, there are only ever three reasons to hire a coach, no matter what business you're in.

1. When you're stuck.
2. When you've plateaued.
3. When you're moving backwards.

Not only do I advocate coaching only for the above three situations, but I also don't recommend working with a coach weekly or monthly. That includes when or if you're working with me.

Just take what I've given you, run with it, and when you begin to plateau or slip backwards, give me a call. You should never become an annuity for a coach where you're just giving them money month after month. That includes me.

There is a reason personal coaching is the ninth step in my system rather than the first. A lot of business success systems out there *begin* with coaching. But I'd rather you do the personal coaching at the end instead of the beginning because I've found that coaching is more effective if you have already been at this a while and have simply run into a snag somewhere along the way, rather than a beginner who needs someone to hold their hand to start the process. Most people who start out that way grow dependent on their coach, where they can't do anything without them. That's a bad place to be.

How do you measure the effectiveness of a coach?

Are they accomplishing what you want to accomplish? How much money are they making? If they're not where you want to be, and they're making more money as a coach than as a VO artist, keep looking.

Are you making progress with their advice or just spinning your wheels? If it's the latter, it's time to move on to another coach.

How my coaching program works.

My coaching method is a hybrid model combining personal and group coaching. This is more cost effective and has a broader range of additional resources, because you're sharing with other people who are on the same journey as you. Then, as you need it, you can get access to additional one-on-one coaching. You also get the coaching you need when you need it, and you're not paying for anything that doesn't benefit you.

What do I mean by hybrid model?

In my system you can get one-on-one coaching within a group context. I'll give you an example to illustrate how that works. Every week, during a group coaching call, I ask if students have a script that they'd like to read and get feedback. It's a group call, but students get some personalized, one-on-one feedback on their performance directly from me.

But again, the way this program works is you do the coaching at the end, when and if you need it. I don't know what you'll need help with. Neither do you. You might be really great at the marketing and get a lot of clients right at the start, but your performance or editing may need a little work. Or you might plateau at a particular income threshold and can't go over that.

The truth is, anyone who wants to be a success in VO can do so. And I've given you all the tools you need right here in this book so you can do that.

But if you need some personal coaching to get you over a rough spot, I can do that too.

If you're still not sure if VO is for you, or you want to take me up on some coaching, visit www.CanYouDoVO.com to see if VO coaching is right for you.

That's it. You've gone through all the steps in my nine-step VO Blueprint system. Congratulations!

There's just one more thing. Remember earlier when I said we were going to go more in depth about the world of audiobook narration? Well read on. That special bonus chapter is next.

SPECIAL BONUS CHAPTER: AUDIOBOOK NARRATION

Remember earlier when I said we'd talk about more in depth about audiobooks? Well here is that section. An entire special bonus chapter in fact.

I've only recorded 41 audiobooks to date. I say "only" because there are those, far more experienced than me, that recorded hundreds (and even thousands) of audiobooks.

Most of my clients hire me for corporate related projects. While I record commercials, video game characters (on occasion), on-hold messages, etc., audiobooks hold a special place in my heart.

The reason I feel this way is because audiobooks helped to keep my VO business afloat in the early years. I almost always had an audiobook in production early on to make sure I was always generating income.

I also believe that audiobooks should be a primary area of focus when you're first getting started in VO.

You need all the experience you can get when you're just getting started, and audiobooks provide that in spades! Not just in terms of narration, but also editing. Recording a book takes many hours, and you'll have ample opportunity to edit out lots of "ums" and "uhs" and your neighbor's dog barking at the Amazon Prime van.

And since I want this book to be the greatest resource for freelance VO artists on the planet, I've gotten a little help for this chapter from my friend of 30 years, Tom Parks. Tom is a former pastor turned audiobook narrator who has recorded hundreds of audiobooks and makes a full-time, multiple six-figure income doing so. But since Tom has far more audiobook experience that I do (and tells it so much better than I can), I'll let him take over from here.

All right. Let's get into audiobook narration. Take it away, Tom.

Hi. Tom Parks here. Bill gave me a kind introduction, so I won't elaborate on it much here, except to share a bit more about my background.

I've been doing audiobooks since 2009. I'm now involved in a lot of different facets of the audiobook industry. I narrate as well as do some producing. Not only do I hire talent to produce books for publishers, but I also have 17 audiobook proofers who listen to recordings of audiobooks and catch errors and make sure names and words are pronounced correctly, as well as five audio engineers who do editing. We edit other narrators' files as well as books that I narrate. This is my full-time gig and I feel very fortunate to have this job, but it all started rather by accident.

Before my life as an audiobook narrator began, I was in pastoral ministry for almost 25 years and kind of stumbled into audiobooks. I was pastoring at a church in Michigan where I lived at the time, and a woman in my church was looking for a job. She interviewed to be a receptionist for a place called Brilliance Audio. While in the interview, a woman came running in with an armload of what turned out to be audiobooks and said, "I need somebody who can record all these audiobooks. Do you know anyone?"

"I think my pastor could do it," my parishioner replied, and gave the woman my phone number.

Next thing I know, I'm getting a call from this producer asking for me to send them a demo. Now, I had no idea what went into producing audiobooks and no inkling what a demo was, but I told her, "Sure," and got to work.

I got on Uncle Google to figure out what a demo was, then read a chapter of *Blue Like Jazz* by Donald Miller into a Zoom recorder, transferred it to a CD (remember those?) and mailed it in. Then I didn't hear anything for a year.

I forgot about the whole experience and went on with my life. Then one night, out of the blue, I got a call from a producer who had finally listened to my demo and wanted me to come in and do some auditions. That led to me doing my first four books for them, a YA title and three nonfiction titles. And I learned that Brilliance Audio, which I had never heard of, was the second largest audiobook producer in the world, owned by Amazon.

I averaged doing one audiobook about every other month for them, all in studio. Over the next 7-8 months I did some religious nonfiction for them, drawing on my background as a pastor.

Then Christian publisher Zondervan, who had heard some of my work, wanted me to narrate a book about the Biblical prophet Hosea. The original narrator they had hired wasn't working out—he pronounced the prophet's name Jose or something—and they knew from my background and the work I had done thus far that I could do a good job for them.

For the next two years I recorded audiobooks in my master bedroom closet. Then audiobooks exploded when Audible said they wanted to record every book ever written. I resigned from the church to narrate audiobooks full time, and the rest, as they say, his history.

Today I make $350,000 a year recording audiobooks, and I can't imagine doing anything else. Bill kindly invited me here to tell you how you can narrate and record audiobooks too.

Let's get started.

What Is an Audiobook?

This may seem like a no-brainer, but let's examine it for a moment. I define audiobooks this way: Communicating someone else's words and telling that story in a compelling way that makes it come alive in a listener's imagination so that they can picture themselves in that situation.

Audiobooks are an intimate medium, as well as a very old one. The first form of storytelling was oral, and all of mankind's oldest tales, from the Bible to Beowulf, were passed down in the oral tradition for centuries before finally being written down.

What Makes Audiobook Narration Different from Other VO Gigs?

With audiobooks it's about more than just the voice. It's about the performance. Can you tell a story and keep a listener engaged over a lengthy period of time? Can you keep up the same level of energy over a 19 1/2 hour audiobook?

As stated above, audiobooks are very intimate. Most audiobook listeners are doing so in their car or via earbuds while doing laundry or some other task. They are in an intimate relationship with the narrator reading the book. Your voice carries the book's words into their living rooms and into their personal lives. You're speaking to them directly, right where they are. That's intimate. That's powerful.

Audiobook narration allows you to talk in a more normal voice than you can when doing a 30-second commercial, where you're yelling or communicating at a high energy level for the entire length of the piece.

With audiobooks, you're not selling anything as you are when narrating a commercial. You're simply telling a story. You're engaging in very simple conversation as you would with a close friend.

The Growth of the Audiobook Industry

The audiobook industry is blowing up. Sales of audiobooks grew 25% in 2021, compared to just 12% in 2020. Audiobooks are predicted to become a $19 billion industry by 2027.

Suffice it to say this is an industry with a lot of potential. And you can position yourself to reap the benefits.

One major thing that happened recently in the audiobook industry is music and podcast streaming app Spotify's purchase of audiobook producer Findaway Voices (more on them below). Spotify wants to get into the audiobook business in a big way by creating a huge audiobook library exclusive to their platform. Over the next five years, they are poised to invest $25-$30 billion to produce new titles. That's billion with a B. Incredible. That's a huge opportunity for you, the savvy audiobook narrator.

How Much do Audiobook Narrators Earn?

That's the big question you're probably asking yourself, right? On ACX, which is *the* audiobook narration marketplace, narrators get paid anywhere from $50-$100 per finished hour (PFH) on the low end. Trained actors who are members of SAG-AFTRA, get $175 PFH and up for union-contracted work. But if you're just starting out, $50-$100 PFH is a good place to start. Just keep in mind that once you get a couple of audiobooks under your belt you'll want to raise your rates, because most big audiobook publishers will think your cheap rates means you aren't that good and they won't hire you.

Note that this rate is per *finished* hour. That means the audio is as perfect as can be and is free of any and all flubs, interruptions and background noise. It takes me around two hours to get one hour of finished audio, but it can take more if you're just getting started, like maybe between four and six hours, on average. For a 100,000 word audiobook, that comes out to between 44-66 hours per book.

You can always do shorter books. I narrate nonfiction pretty much exclusively, which tends to run shorter than most fiction novels. Most of the books I do end up being between 6 and 7 hours. I shoot for 4 1/2 hours of finished audio per day, which takes me about 7 hours to do. I'll typically record for a couple of hours, take a break, do two more hours, and so on until I've reached my allotted 4 1/2 hours for the day.

You won't start out making $350k right out of the gate. It took me ten years to reach that level. But with a little discipline and some hard work you can get there.

If you'd like to start your audiobook narration journey today, check out my online course at AudiobookSeminar.com

Payment or Royalty Share?

ACX will also allow you to do a royalty share with the author. This means that you don't make any money right away, but you could potentially get royalties off of sales of the completed audiobook. We'll talk more about ACX and royalty share a bit later.

The Many Types of Audiobooks

As you can probably already guess, the bulk of the audiobook market is made up of fiction. Fiction outsells nonfiction, but nonfiction is also gaining in popularity as people seek to improve their lives and grow their skillsets.

In the fiction category, the biggest genres in the audiobook field are Romance, Sci-Fi/Fantasy, and Young Adult (YA). The same is true in the print and eBook worlds. If you can do any of these genres well you can write your own ticket. By far the largest of these categories in audiobooks is Sci-Fi/ Fantasy, with Mysteries/Thrillers/Suspense a close second. Romance was up 75% in 2021.

In the non-fiction category, some of the biggest categories include science and tech, faith-based, philosophy, business, and abstracts. Abstracts are where people take longer works, like *The Ten-Minute Manager* or *How to Win Friends and Influence People*, and turn them into short 15-20 minute audio summaries.

If you are looking for a real growth opportunity and the subject matter doesn't turn you off, porn/erotica is also a huge audiobook category. I'm not kidding.

Choosing Your Niche

Because of my background as a minister, I do a lot of faith-based nonfiction. It's a great niche that has served me well, and it suits my background and interests.

When you're just starting out, think about where you can find your audiobook niche. Maybe you're a huge science fiction fan, or you can't put down a good Amish romance. Yes, I said Amish romance. That is actually a thing.

There is an audiobook genre for every single person reading this. Just as their is for every reader and audiobook listener.

How Do I Tell if audiobooks are a Good Fit For Me?

Some people become enamored with the audiobook industry because they are readers. You get paid to read, right? But there is more to it than that. Audiobook narration takes a lot of time and dedication, not just while you're actively recording in the booth, but prep time beforehand.

So how do you tell if audiobook narration is right for you?

The Closet Test

Before you devote your life to attracting audio producers, see if you can pass what I call the Closet Test.

Get two books from your bookshelf, one you like a lot, and one you can't stand. Now go into your closet and read them aloud cover to cover. Yes, that means all the way through.

If you can get through them you probably have a future in audiobooks. If you get six pages in before giving up, you probably won't make it as an audiobook narrator.

And hey, that's OK. You probably like short-form stuff better. Go back to doing VO for commercials. No harm, no foul.

But to do audiobooks you need to maintain your focus for a long period of time.

OK, so you were able to read *Game of Thrones* aloud to yourself without running away screaming. Now you're ready to build your demo and seek audiobook fame and fortune, right?

Not quite. We still have some prep work left to do. But don't worry. This will be fun, I promise.

Networking with Audiobook Narrators

Networking is an important component of success in just about every industry, and it's no different with audiobooks. Especially since most narration these days is done in our individual homes in isolation.

Don't worry. We don't bite. Audiobook narration is a friendly, non-competitive industry. Most narrators are friends who do things together. We get to know each other's strengths and weaknesses, and we're cognizant of the concept of "paying it forward." In other words, someone helped us get to where we are, and it is our duty to try and return the favor. If we encounter an audio project we can't do, chances are we know someone who can and will gladly refer that producer on to them.

So where do you meet other audiobook narrators?

As with most everything else these days, start your search online.

Facebook Groups for Audio Narrators

Facebook has tons of groups for audiobook narrators. Here are a few good ones:

Facebook.com/groups/audiobookcrowd

Facebook.com/groups/booknarrators

Facebook.com/groups/ACXNarratorsProducers

Facebook.com/AudiobookCreationExchangeNarrators

There may be even more groups by the time you read this. Do a Facebook group search for "audio book narrators" and you will find tons more groups.

These are all great places, especially for beginners. Go check them out. Strike up a conversation with a few of them. You never know where it may lead.

Use the group's search feature to search for a question you want to ask before you ask it. It might have been asked by someone else before you. Don't be a pest or a jerk. Don't offer your services right out of the gate. Remember, at this early stage of the game you are there to learn and make connections.

Now that you're networking with other audiobook professionals, let's take a look at where you should go to actually start getting audiobook narration work.

ACX

ACX.com is an audiobook production marketplace where authors can connect with audio producers. It used to be the main place to find audiobook work, but it is no longer the end all-be all it once was. It now has garbage scripts written by bots used to fool people into parting with their Audible credits so these scammers make money. It's still a good place to find work but you have to be wary of scammers.

In one particular example I heard about, someone who posted a listing for an audiobook of the classic science fiction novel *Dune*. An experienced narrator saw it and signed on to do it, spending hundreds of hours recording and editing it. The finished book ended up being 40 hours long. The narrator made no money up front to do it, and spent a month recording it before paying for someone to professionally master it.

There was just one problem. The person who put the offer on ACX wasn't the rights holder, and when ACX found out they took it down. But not before this narrator had spent all that time, energy, and labor on something he could never get paid for.

This poor narrator not only lost a month of his life and the money he spent on mastering, but he lost out on other paying work he couldn't do because he was working on this scam project.

Don't let that happen to you. You have to be careful. Do your due diligence. If something looks to good to be true, it probably is. Do a little research to find out if the person requesting the audiobook actually has the rights to publish it. Especially if it's a famous book that has been around awhile, like *Dune*.

Also keep in mind that major books in big franchises, like *Star Wars*, *Star Trek*, or *Game of Thrones* are going to be done by their publishers in-house by experienced narrators, and you're never going to see a royalty share deal on ACX to do the latest *Star Trek* novel. If you do, run away.

You should also run away if you see jobs offering crazy high rates like $400 PFH. If you see those, run away as fast as you can.

Now, I'm not saying you should avoid ACX altogether. You should definitely have an ACX account. There is a lot of legitimate work to be found there. Just be aware and be careful.

I'm really not knocking ACX. There are some very good resources there, especially if you're a beginner.

At the top of the ACX home page, click on Production Resources. You'll find a treasure trove for beginning audiobook narrators.

Audiolab - This is a tool that gives you instant feedback on your audio quality at any time. You can use it before you submit auditions, when you're calibrating new equipment, and to check your completed productions to make sure your sound meets their submission requirements. Audiolab gives you the opportunity to record something, upload a file, and they will listen to it and give you a free evaluation to tell you how it sounds.

Submission Requirements - Self-explanatory. This page gives you everything you need to know in order to submit audio that meets ACX's standards.

Audio Terminology Glossary - Every industry has its own technical jargon, and audiobooks are no different. Learning the terminology will help you talk to producers and calibrate your equipment effectively.

Video Lessons and Resources - Even if you never get a single job through ACX I urge you to make use of these video lessons. It's like taking a complete audio production course for free.

There is also a YouTube channel: Youtube.com/user/AudibleACX. This has lots of videos for narrators and producers as well as authors.

Better Than ACX

As cool as ACX is, even with all its flaws, there is a site that is even better. It's called Findaway Voices (FindawayVoices.com).

Findaway's interface is more intuitive than ACX, and there are more producers from legitimate companies who are using Findaway to produce titles. I've done work for big name publishers like Penguin Random House and HarperCollins through Findaway.

You can set your rate or range you want to get paid, as well as see what titles are being offered for auditions. Findaway also lets you keep track of the audiobooks you have produced through their platform, and producers and authors can see this information as well. It helps you market yourself.

And last but not least, Findaway's royalty share program is more fair than ACX.

So by all means set up a profile on ACX and take advantage of their many wonderful educational resources. But set up your profile on Findaway Voices as well. You won't regret it.

Audiobook Narration and AI

At this point you might be wondering about AI voice narration. The technology has improved a lot, and you've probably heard some AI commercial narration. I know I have.

But here's the thing. Right now it's still easy to tell it's an AI rather than a human voice. Will that always be the case? Probably not.

But sophisticated, human-sounding AI will likely hit the low-paying end of the industry first. The kind of stuff that you would pass over anyway once you got a few audiobook projects under your belt. It will also probably impact the nonfiction field before it moves into fiction. This is a concern for me, because I primarily do nonfiction. I might have to make the transition into doing more fiction to keep working.

But I estimate we're still five to ten years away from an AI being able to do a credible—unable to tell it's not a human—job on a really good book. But there are many not-so-good books out there right now that AI could probably narrate just fine. Bottom feeder nonfiction books that the authors or publishers will employ AI in order to get an audiobook produced on the cheap. This is where AI will start planting a foothold.

But no matter what happens with AI, I want you to keep something very important in mind.

As AI spreads, personhood and personability will become even more important. Your unique individualism is what's most important in marketing yourself as an audiobook narrator.

What makes you unique? What do you bring to this industry that no one else can offer?

To be a successful audiobook narrator you must find points of connection between your life and the audio work you want to do. What do you like? What are your interests and hobbies?

What skills do you have? Do you know other languages? Can you do accents or character voices?

Do you have an acting or theater background? Are you an explainer? A teacher?

For example, my background in ministry makes me uniquely suited for doing not only nonfiction in general but religious books in particular. I find religious subjects fascinating, which makes doing those kinds of books a lot of fun. It also makes research easier. Producers love working with me because they know my familiarity with the subject matter will make for a smooth and accurate experience.

So what specialties do you bring to the audio booth? Figuring out and clarifying your core value will not only help you compete against other narrators, but eventually AI.

No matter what happens with AI, I am convinced that there will always be a place for the human voice. If you can master the craft and distinguish yourself you will always do a better job than even the most sophisticated artificial intelligence.

How to Get Work

Now we're getting into the good stuff, the meat and potatoes of this chapter. I'm going to start by telling you some secrets.

Some things that professional audiobook narrators know that you don't.

The Difference Between a Demo and an Audition

Sometimes you're going to be asked for demos and sometimes for auditions. But what's the difference?

Demos are samples you record to get work. Auditions are something producers have you do once they've heard and liked your demo. You record demos on your own; you are asked to record auditions.

Let's start with demos.

Bill has already explained how to record a great demo, but demos for audiobooks are a little different from commercial demos.

For example, it's common in commercial demos to begin each one with your name and the type of narration you're doing. For example, "Tom Parks. Sports narration." This is called a slate.

With audiobook demos you don't need to do that. It isn't wrong, it's just that nobody does it. Audiobook producers aren't used to hearing it, so when you add a slate to your audiobook demo it's jarring to them.

Keep your audiobook demos short and immediately compelling. Use 4-5 pieces, each one around 1-2 minutes in length. Find an excerpt from what you're recording that's going to jump out and shows them what you are capable of from the very beginning. Something that makes them lean forward and say, "Man, I wish they had kept going."

You want to make them want to know more about it. You want them to stop multitasking and listen to you.

You don't have to start with chapter one, page one. For fiction, jump right into the action. Give them some dialogue and establish characters quickly early on. Feature any accents or dialects you're really good at. Remember that with dialects and accents the producer wants to hear that you can make them sound authentic and not cartoony. You need to know the difference between an Irish brogue and a Scottish brogue. Don't overdo the accents.

The more characters you can work in during a demo the better. Make the characters unique from one another. Show them doing some compelling action or having a dramatic conversation. You need to demonstrate to the producer that you can keep those characters straight. Show their emotions.

In nonfiction, you want to be confident and conversational. Sound like you are talking to the listener. Be matter-of-fact.

Whatever the genre or subject matter, make it your best work. There are no do-overs with producers. You only have a couple of minutes to grab them and make them pay attention.

Make sure the audio for your demos and auditions is as clean as you can make it. Producers aren't just listening to your performance. They are also listening to your noise floor, your microphone, your room, and your EQ. This has to be as good as a finished audiobook ready for sale.

Producers make a decision within the first 30 seconds of the first track you send them. Lead off with your best work. Don't save the best for last.

Support materials. We don't send out physical auditions anymore, but that doesn't mean we can skimp on the packaging. What can you say in the first line of your email to producers that grabs their attention and makes them want to drop whatever they're doing and download your demo? Don't try to sell the material. Be careful not to over-hype or oversell. Just perform really well and put your best work out there.

Identify early on in an email why you are unique. "I grew up reading stories to my GI Joes," or "I spent 15 years in Italy and speak Italian like a native" is better than "Hi, I'm Tom Parks and I hope you like my demo." Think creative and unusual. Producers get between 500 and one thousand demos a year. That's per producer, not over the entire publisher. Find a way to stand out.

Label the demo itself to call out why it's unique. "Male-Female Sci-Fi British accent demo" is better than "Parks Demo YA 3-Character Action Scene." Tell the producers what they're listening to. For example, "Two sisters Amish Romance Scene." This shows that you have the awareness that you know what you are doing is unique.

It is important that you build up your audiobook portfolio. Most producers are looking for you to have 25-30 titles for sale in the genre you are demoing for. The more work you do, the easier it will be for you to get more work.

Don't be afraid to send your demo multiple times to the same producer. Audiobook producers are extremely busy. They forget. They lose your demo, or your email got stuck in their spam folder.

I sent my demo to Tantor Media 17 times over a three-year period before they finally hired me. So be patient and follow up. Just because you haven't heard back from them doesn't mean they think you stink. It's more likely that they haven't had a chance to listen to your demo at all. So keep checking back.

As I have already pointed out, producers get a *lot* of demos. You are throwing your hat in the ring with a lot of other people who are trying to do this work. But producers are always looking for new talent, the next fresh voice. They are always actively looking for people just like you.

With auditions, you have been asked by a producer to give them a sample performance. This is great news! It means you're almost there.

The trick with auditions is to give producers exactly what they asked for, no more and no less. If they ask for the first two pages, then give them just the first two pages. Even if the second page ends mid-sentence.

Sometimes, if they know you and are confident that you know what you're doing, they will want a raw read with no mastering.

As with demos, make sure your audition reflects your best quality performance. Read it as if you've actually got the gig and people are going to be paying to hear this. Think to yourself, "How would I perform this if I got the gig?"

This isn't a throwaway thing you're doing just to do it. Put some thought and effort into it. How do you really want it to sound?

Do some background research on the title and the author. Make sure you know how to pronounce the author's last name correctly.

Turn around the audition quickly. No one expects it immediately after they asked for it, but don't let it sit for three or four days either.

Don't get discouraged. Keep in mind that getting asked to audition is huge! When producers ask you to audition you've already made it. They want to put you up alongside other qualified narrators in order to decide who they want to do the project. If you don't get picked to do that book, you might get chosen to do the next one.

You won't get every book you audition for. Just keep working at getting work and you'll be fine.

Connecting with the Audiobook Industry

While you're sending out demos and recording auditions, make some time to connect with the audiobook industry as a whole. It's very friendly and welcoming, and you'll learn a lot about the art, craft, and business of audiobook production that will only help you stand out and become a better narrator.

Audio Publishers Association (Audiopub.org) is the official voice of the industry. They host an annual conference (APAC) as well as the Audie Awards. There is a member directory as well as tons of learning resources.

The conference is a lot of fun. There are classes and workshops, as well as networking opportunities.

SAG/AFTRA, or Screen Actors Guild-American Federation of Television and Radio Artists, is a union representing film and television actors, radio personalities, and audiobook narrators like you. They provide benefits like health insurance and pensions for people who narrate books covered by their contrats.

Social Media

Authors and publishers—especially authors—expect you to help sell their products. If you're hired directly by an author there's an expectation that you're going to help market their book. This means announcing the book on your social media platform to your followers and fans if you have any.

Indie authors especially use social media as their primary marketing tool, and they hope you will help them sell their products. That means that in addition to voice talent, they will be looking for narrators who have a large social media following.

I don't do a lot on social media, I do more books directly for publishers and don't do many projects directly with authors. But if an author gets two narrators they like equally well, the one with a big social media following will get the edge.

To them, more followers equals more buyers. So if you decide to aggressively pursue the ACX royalty share model, you'll want to be active on social media.

With social media, the number one rule is go where your prospects are. If you're specializing in nonfiction business titles, you'll want to be active on Twitter and LinkedIn. If Amish romance is more your thing, Instagram and Facebook are where you want to be.

Bill mentioned websites earlier, and he has a great one. But he specializes in commercial VO work. I don't have a website. If you build a body of work on Audible and Findaway Voices, that's where producers will find you and listen to your clips. You'll also get reader/listener feedback, and you'll come up in search results when producers and authors go on these platforms looking for a narrator.

In terms of getting more work, I have yet to see a website as being terribly effective. For every person who got work from a website there are thousands who built websites and got very little if any traction.

If you want to have one, that's great. Just don't spend a lot of money on it. Make it simple and fun and easy to update and manage. And make sure people can find you and your work on audiobook websites like ACX and Findaway Voices.

Nailing the Process of Narrating Audiobooks

Whether you want to do audiobooks as part of a mix with other VO work, or you want to pursue them exclusively, you'll need to set up a workflow and a process for actually getting your audiobook narration done.

Here's my process. Your situation is different. You will need to come up with your own, something that works best for you and who you are as a person and as a narrator.

My process is kind of unique in that I'm an early morning person. I'm a workaholic, but I'm also newly married (January 1st, 2021) and we live in a beach community. Both of these factors impact how I live my life and run my business.

I get up at 4:15 in the morning and make coffee. Then I do some readings, check the news, play with my cat, and warm up my voice as well as my brain, engaging my critical thinking skills before I go into the studio.

Before I start recording I listen to the last few minutes that I recorded the previous day to remember where I was and match the tone and style. I'm usually recording between 4:45 and 5am.

My wife gets up at 8, so I take a break and we go for a walk. I then go back into the booth and record some more. By 10am my day is half done. I take another break at that time.

By lunch I'm done recording for the day. I take a break at 1:30, take a nap or go grocery shopping.

The afternoons are for marketing and administrative tasks. I pay my engineers, as well as bill clients for my work. I also contact publishers. This stuff takes place between 3 and 5pm. At 5:30 I'm done for the day.

If we're going to the beach that day, I work until 9 or 9:15, then we head to the beach. We get home by 2pm and I work the rest of the day, doing administrative tasks in the evening.

I only work on one audiobook at a time. I just don't have the bandwidth for multiple projects at the same time. The only thing I might be doing is reading and researching the next book I'm going to be working on. But I'm only recording one book at a time.

That's how I plan *my* day. You lead a different life than I do and your day might be different. You might have small children or other responsibilities. The key is to design a schedule that works best for you, and freelance audiobook narration, and VO work in general, allows you to do that wonderfully.

Equipment and Software

Bill has already discussed microphones, computers, and software, but I'll tell you what I use and recommend for my audiobook narration business.

As for computers, I'm a big PC guy. What you have already is probably good enough. It just needs to be powerful enough and fast enough that the digital audio workstation (DAW) you want to use can run on it. I use the Focusrite Scarlet interface for connecting my microphone to my computer.

I'm a "less is more" kind of guy. I don't do any EQ, gating, limiting, or compressing when I'm recording. I just want to record the most quiet and transparent audio file I can get. The editor and producer can usually add all that stuff later, but they can't remove it if there's too much to start with without ruining the audio quality.

Microphones. I find that USB mics still aren't quite there yet. They introduce extraneous noise into the signal chain. Avoid dynamic mics as well, as they can also be noisy. I don't use a pop filter. You actually don't need one if you position your microphone correctly.

Software. I use Pro Tools. Why? Because I use Pro Tools. It's what I've always used. There are tons of DAWs on the market, many of them even free, and they all get the job done to an equal or lesser degree. When shopping around for a DAW, I suggest selecting one that supports punch and roll editing.

What is punch and roll editing? It's a recording method that allows you to go back and fix errors you make during your recording sessions while you are actively recording. You're going to flub something during a reading, even if you're warmed up and have read the text beforehand.

With punch and roll, when you mess up you can pause the recording, back up over the mistake, redo it, and then continue on with your recording session.

I love this method of editing because it keeps me in the moment. I don't have to go back later after I've recorded the entire book and look for each mistake, and I can deliver the correction with the same tone and intent as the preceding section. It makes recording faster so that I get more done each day.

My producers love it because it makes the files easier to edit. They can edit a 5-hour section of my audio in 20 minutes.

So find a DAW that supports punch and roll editing and give it a try. I think you'll like it. Pro Tools has it, as does Audacity and several others, and there are tons of videos online for how to do punch and roll editing in your particular software.

For reading manuscripts in the booth, I use an IPad. There's no sound of turning pages for the mic to pick up, and I can leave notes for the editors and proofers right on the manuscript.

Manuscript Preparation

Before you begin recording a book, read it carefully cover to cover first. Look up how to pronounce certain character names or made-up words, or ask the author how to say something. This is especially important in science fiction and fantasy novels, but it goes for foreign words and phrases as well.

Make note of any special accents the characters might have as well.

I'll provide a cautionary tale to drive home why this is so important. Legendary audiobook narrator Dick Hill was doing a 730-page, 70-hour audiobook once without prepping first. He just dove in and started reading it.

His wife was his engineer. He got to the last chapter when he realized the main character had a Scottish brogue. It took him longer to rerecord that one character's lines than it did to record the entire book! He would have saved himself hundreds of hours of work by simply reading the book first.

Research Tools

Merriam-Webster.com is an important resource, especially for U.S. audiobook publishers. British publishers will ask you to use the Oxford English Dictionary (OED.com).

Forvo.com is the go-to resource for native pronounciations of foreign words, like French towns for example. You can listen in French or English.

Youglish.com searches for videos where words are pronounced. It will even take you to the exact spot in the video where the word is spoken.

OK. That's my "how to get into the audiobook narration business" spiel. Now I'm going to share with you the secrets for staying in it, and becoming one of the best narrators in the industry. Are you ready? Because this is really powerful stuff.

Here goes.

Treat it Like a Business

This should go without saying, but you'd be surprised how many talented audiobook narrators mess up this crucial step.

One time I was speaking at an audiobook narrator conference and there was a debate about what we should call ourselves. Are we narrators or performers? People on both sides of the issue raised some good points, and everyone was very passionate about it one way or the other. But I gave it some thought and scrapped the presentation I was going to do and wrote a new one.

In it I suggested we were neither narrators nor performers. Instead we are small business owners who provide services to the audiobook community.

Think of yourself as a small business owner, because at the end of the day that's what you are. If you only focus on the narration you're going to miss a lot of important stuff. Stuff like...

Taxes. Should you pay them yearly or quarterly? How can you structure your business to pay as little as possible? Get a good accountant who has worked with small freelance business owners like yourself and knows whether or not you should file as self-employed, an S-Corp, a C-Corp, or an LLC.

This will cost money, but it will save you even more money in the long run. I pay my accountant $700 a year, but he saves me $6,000-$7,000 a year in taxes.

Are you protected in case you get sued? It sounds far-fetched in the world of audiobooks, but it could happen. I narrated for this "doctor" once who wrote a lot of wacky self-help stuff. I didn't want to get sued if he was sued for malpractice, so I had a lawyer draw up a contract that protects me from liability in case that happens. Fortunately, it hasn't happened. But I'm protected just in case it does.

A good attorney and accountant are worth their weight in gold for your business. Investing in them now will save you tons of time, money, and headaches later.

Time. What is your real time hourly rate that you're getting paid, especially on royalty share deals? Time is money. Keep accurate track of your time and develop ways to tighten up the time you spend recording in the booth.

While you're tracking your time, don't forget to consider what is the best use of your time. Your time is best suited to doing two things: Recording audiobooks and finding more audiobooks to record.

I discovered early on that while editing, proofing, and mastering are important, they are not the best, most productive use of my time. I'm not good at any of them. I don't have those skills or the training, and so doing it would take too much time that would be better spent recording audiobooks and finding more audiobooks to record.

That is why I have built up a network of people who know how to do those things. My least experienced editor has done 1,000 titles. And because I have a group of people who can edit and proof audiobooks some companies pay me just to read, while others pay me to do the full production.
I have a good relationship with talented people who know I will pay them the going rate or better, and can do good work. It's well worth it to pay $75 PFH to someone else instead of doing it myself. If I can send it off to an editor to proof I can be recording another book or finding more work.

If I'm editing and proofing a book I'm not recording another one or finding more work.

Now, if you're good at editing and fast, keep doing it. If not you should farm it out.

Begin with the End in Mind

I learned this from Stephen Covey, and it has served me well these last ten years. Whatever you set out to do, start with the end result in mind. You want to be an audiobook narrator? Great. What does that ideal life look like? When you're well established and making money, what does your day, your week, your month look like? Where do you want to be in one year? In five years? In ten? What steps do you need to take right now to attain those goals?

Whatever your ideal career is, whether its VO, audiobooks specifically, or something else, sit down and think about what the end might look like so you can develop a path for how to get there. Plan with the end in mind.

Learn from Others

You don't need paying client work to start becoming a great audiobook narrator. Start by being an audiobook listener. Learn from other people. Become a consumer of audiobooks, especially in the genre you're interested in doing.

Listen to podcasts. I'm a huge fan of This American Life on NPR. It's a great podcast for stories.

Think of listening as part of the work of doing audiobooks. If you want to do commercial VOs, then listening to commercials is part of the work, and you'll probably pay more attention to the commercials than the TV shows you're watching. The same must be equally true of audiobooks.

Listen to Yourself

You also need to learn how to listen to yourself.

Going back and listening to the book you just recorded may be hard but you need to do it. Three to four times a year I go back and listen to an entire book I've done from beginning to end just as you would any other audiobook done by someone else. Learn to think critically about your own work.

Did you hold your attention from beginning to end? Did you do a good job with the characters? What can you do better next time? Learn to engage in a little healthy comparison. Take notes while listening to yourself as well as other narrators. Jot down 3-4 bullet points. Focus on one thing you want to get better the next time you record a book.

Give Time Every Day to the Work

If you want to be an audiobook narrator you must devote some time every single day to the work. If you're a writer, you write. If you're a plumber, you plumb. That's just what you do. There's no other way around it. You have to start right now giving time every single day to the work you want to do.

What if you don't have any books scheduled to record? You can grab one off your shelf and record half an hour's worth, then listen to it and critique it. Not just your performance, but the audio quality as well.

I did this when I was first getting started so I could learn to use my microphone and recording software. Then I critiqued myself. Did I sustain the right mood and energy? Were my files clean? My levels consistent?

Doing this practice also gets you used to being in the environment of your recording space and spending that time recording audiobooks.

What else should you spend time on? Well, there's...

Contacting publishers. I spend some time every single day contacting publishers and sending out demos. If you don't hear from some of them, follow up until you do. As your demos improve, send them better demos.

Editing audio. Practice editing audio every single day. If you don't have anything recorded ask for someone else's audio to edit for practice. That's where networking with other narrators comes in handy.

My point is that you must devote time every day to the work as if this is your job and what you want to do, because it will be, and it is.

How much time? That's up to you. As I stated earlier, everyone starts from a different place, and has a different situation.

Set a tangible goal and stick with it. How much time will you give every single day to the attainment of your dream? Will you give an hour a day? Two hours? On your day off, can you give 5-6 hours a day?

Are you going to do it in the morning or evening? Weekends?

I want to hammer these points home because they are applicable to whatever career you're in right now as well. You might not want to narrate audiobooks full time, and that's fine. But set a tangible goal to be the best you can be in whatever career you are in and you will find success.

The 1% Solution

No one is expecting you to be a completely different person by tomorrow night. You don't need to be 100% better at whatever it is you're trying to achieve in order to be successful.

Strive instead to be just 1% better.

Find the time every single day to get 1% better at something, in all areas of your life.

For example, strive to get 1% better physically. I got married in 2021, and my wife is allergic to gluten. I do the cooking and eat what she eats because it's just easier that way. She also walks every day and I walk with her. After the first six months of our marriage I lost 30 pounds!

This 1% improvement of my core strength paid off in the form of benefits in the recording booth. I can now stay in the booth longer without feeling beaten up, and my neck pain is gone.

Strive to get 1% better emotionally. What can you do to handle stress better? Be more relaxed? I get a massage once a week, which helps me be able to record longer.

Strive to improve your performance 1%. I strive every day to be 1% better at audiobook performance. Even if I am narrating a terrible book I want it to be the best work I've ever done.

So work to be 1% better in everything you do, every area of your life, and in a month or a year's time those percentages will really add up to something great.

That's it. Everything I've learned in ten years of being a full-time, six-figure audiobook narrator. If I can do it you can too.

Just treat it like a business, devote time to practice and continual improvement, get better at your craft, and you too can be a successful audiobook narrator.

If you would like to learn more about becoming an audiobook narrator, please check out my audiobook voice over course at AudiobookSeminar.com

CONCLUSION

This is Bill once again . . .

These past 17 years working as a full-time voice over talent has been quite a ride. If you had told me 20 years ago the type of life and life-style I'd be living in a few short years, I'd have told you that you're crazy!

I've learned that building a voice over business (or any business for that matter) is not easy. It takes work, dedication, and persistence.

But I've also learned that the voice business is simple! So simple, in fact, that most anyone who wants to do it, can do so, with the proper training and guidance.

I would love to be YOUR voice over guide, mentor, and coach!

I've provided help to thousands in the arena of voice over. They can testify to the fulfillment they've attained, the freedom they've experienced, and the profit they now have to life the type of life they only dreamed of before.

Are you ready to start your VO journey?

You first step begins at www.CanYouDoVO.com.

Made in the USA
Las Vegas, NV
24 October 2024

10341972R00079